Wapwony Acoli:
LET'S LEARN ACOLI

Mother Tongue Series

DR. MOLLYNN MUGISHA-OTIM
Translated By Dr. Stephen Ojok Otim

AuthorHouse™ UK
1663 Liberty Drive
Bloomington, IN 47403 USA
www.authorhouse.co.uk
Phone: 0800.197.4150

Published by AuthorHouse 02/28/2019

ISBN: 978-1-5462-9592-1 (sc)
ISBN: 978-1-5462-9593-8 (e)

Print information available on the last page.

This book is printed on acid-free paper.

authorHOUSE®

This book is dedicated to my daughter Kayla, who had difficulty finding the Acoli translation of "munchkin"; and my strong footballer son Myrhon; whose desire to learn Acoli inspired me to create this resource.

This map shows parts of Northern Uganda and South Sudan where Acoli speaking people mainly come from.

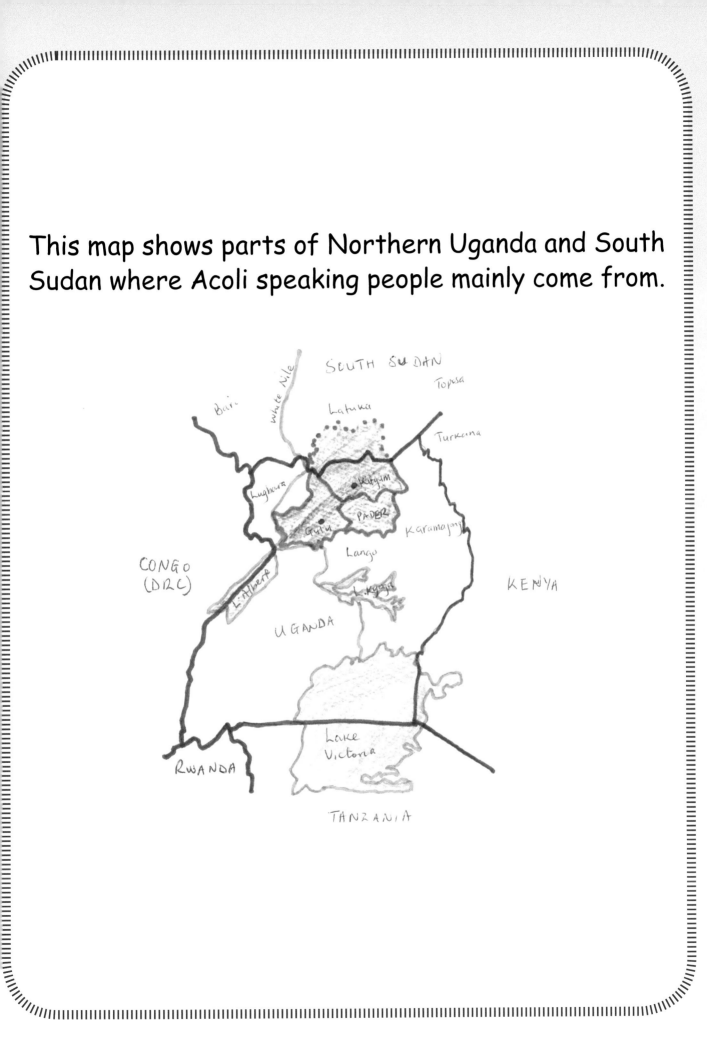

Greeting

Ico nining?
Good morning?

Kop aŋo?
Hello/ How are you?

Wanen.
Goodbye.

Apwoyo.
Welcome/Thank you.

Wanen lacen.
See you later.

But maber.
Good night.

Atye maber.
I am fine.

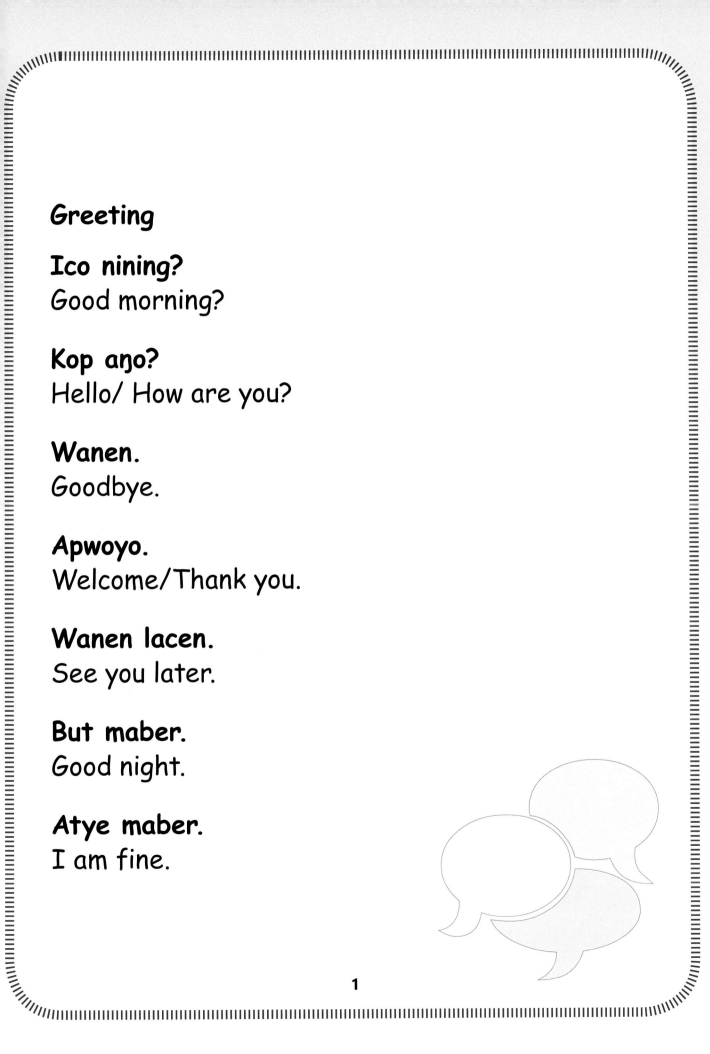

MY BODY

Awobi (Boy)

Wic (Head)

Wang dano (Face)

It (Ear)

Um *(Nose)*

Dog *(Mouth)*

Ciŋ (Hand)

Lwet (Nail)

Waŋ (Eye)

Leb (Tongue)

Lak (Teeth)

Ii (Stomach)

Tyen (Leg)

Nyig Tyen (Toes)

Anyaka (Girl)

Yer *(Hair)*

Gwok *(Shoulder)*

Koma *(Body)*

Bat *(Arm)*

Nyig Ciŋ *(Fingers)*

Atye ki waŋa aryo.
I have 2 eyes.

An awobi.
I am a boy.

An Anyaka.
I am a girl.

Ajwayo laka.
I brush my teeth.

MY FAMILY

Amaro babaa na.
I love my daddy.

Maa mara.
My mummy loves me.

Atye ki lamera matidi acel.
I have 1 younger sister.

Daa na bedo I Uganda.
My grandmother lives in Uganda.

Babaa na tye laco ento Maa tye dako.
My father is a man but my mother is a woman.

OUR HOME

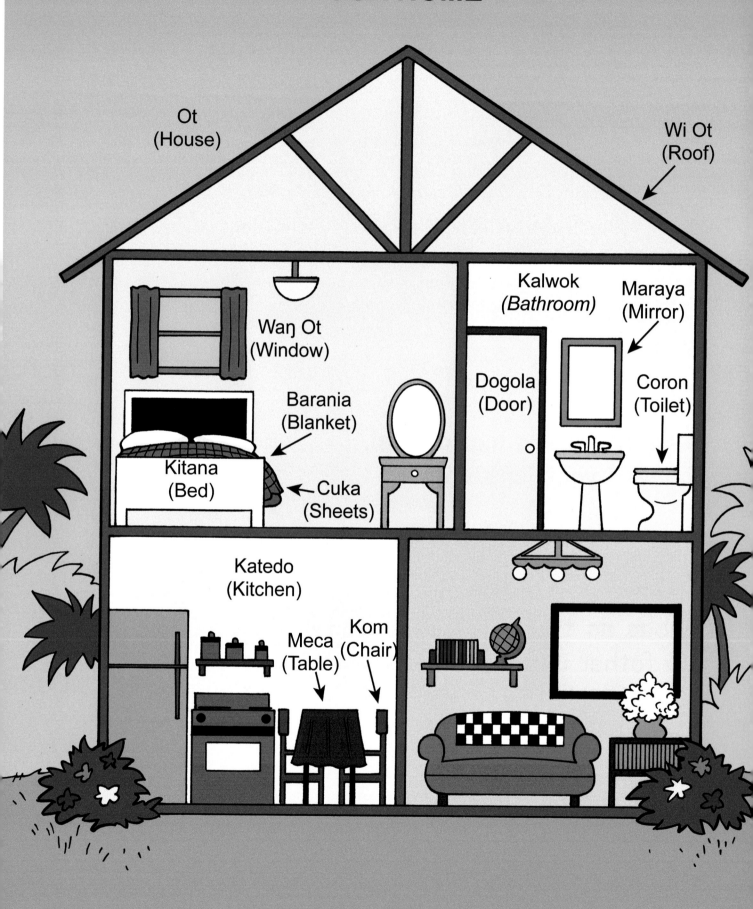

Waŋ ot tye twolo.
The window is open.

Waya tye katedo.
Auntie is cooking.

Cuka wa tar.
Our bedsheets are white.

Dogola ki puŋo.
The door is locked.

ANIMALS

Alworo twol.
I fear snakes.

Pud pe aneno kanna.
I have never seen a horse.

Nera tye ki dyegi mia acel.
My uncle has 100 goats.

Dyang miyo cak.
Cows give milk.

1. Acel

2. Aryo

3. Adek

4. Aŋwen

5. Abic

6. Abicel

7. Abiro

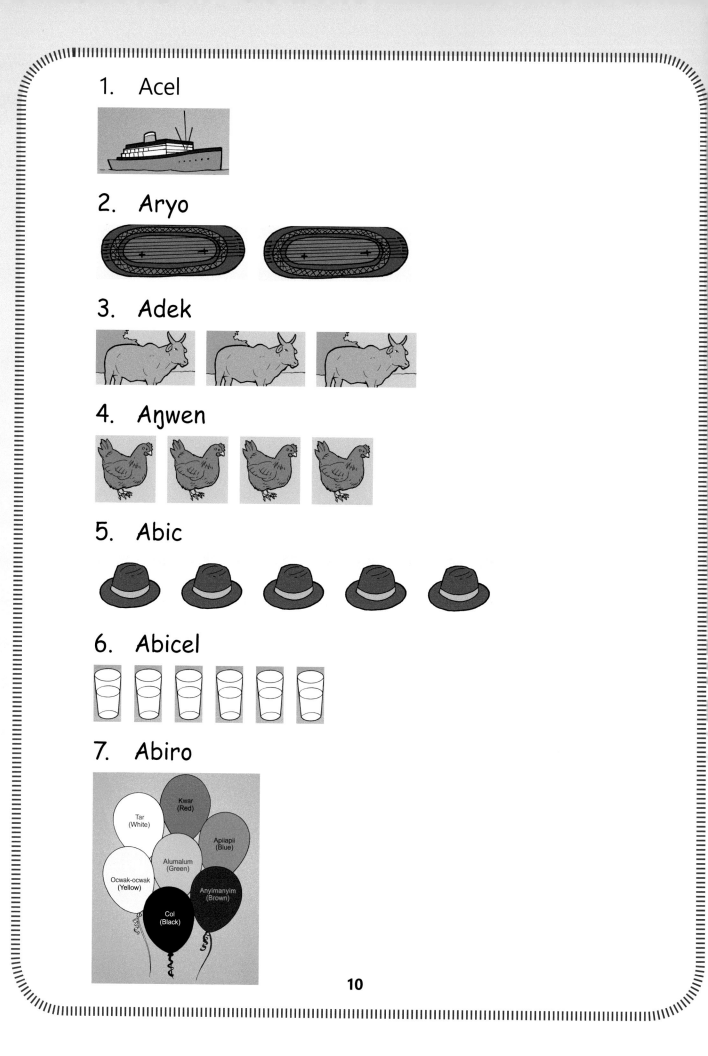

8. Aboro

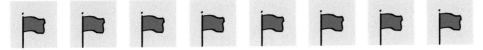

9. Abuŋwen

10. Apar

11. Apar wi acel
12. Apar wi aryo
13. Apar wi adek
14. Apar wi aŋwen
15. Apar wi abic
16. Apar wi abicel
17. Apar wi abiro
18. Apar wi aboro
19. Apar wi abuŋwen
20. Pyer aryo
21. Pyer aryo wi acel
30. Pyer adek
31. Pyer adek wi acel
40. Pyer aŋwen
50. Pyer abic
60. Pyer abicel
70. Pyer abiro
80. Pyer aboro
90. Pyer abuŋwen
100. Mia acel

FOOD

Pii (Water)

Malaga (Spoon)

Cak (Milk)

Tyang (Sugarcane)

Riŋu dyel (Goat Meat)

Riŋu (Beef)

Kikobo (Cup)

Rec (Fish)

Papayi (Pawpaw)

Layata (Sweet Potatoes)

Muyeme (Mangoes)

Mugati (Bread)

Cwan (Plate)

Gweno (Chicken)

Kwon kal

Malakwaŋ

Toŋ Gweno (Eggs)

Layata

Apwoyo tedo.
Thanks for the meal.

Apwoyo cam.
Thanks for eating.

Malakwang mit.
Malakwang is tasty.

Cam ocek.
Food is ready.

COLOURS

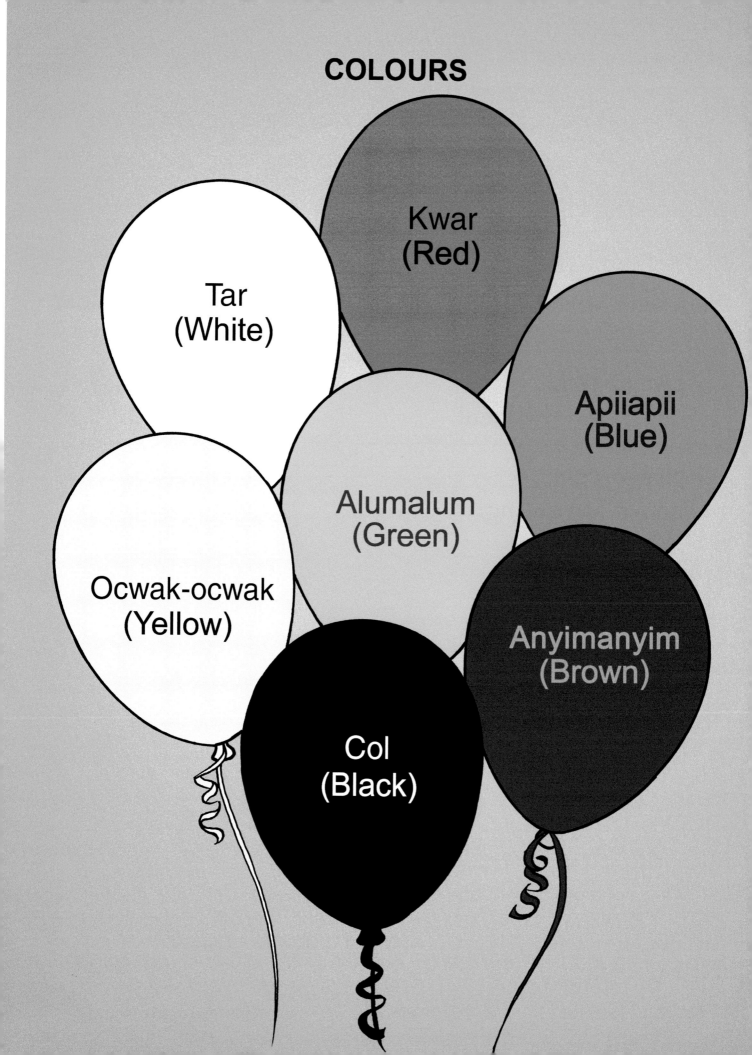

Wamaro romo macol.
We love Black Sheep.

Labolo mucek tye ma ocwak-ocwak.
Ripe bananas are yellow.

Cak tye matar.
Milk is white.

Lamara tye ki tetei makwar.
My cousin has a red dress.

TRAVELLING

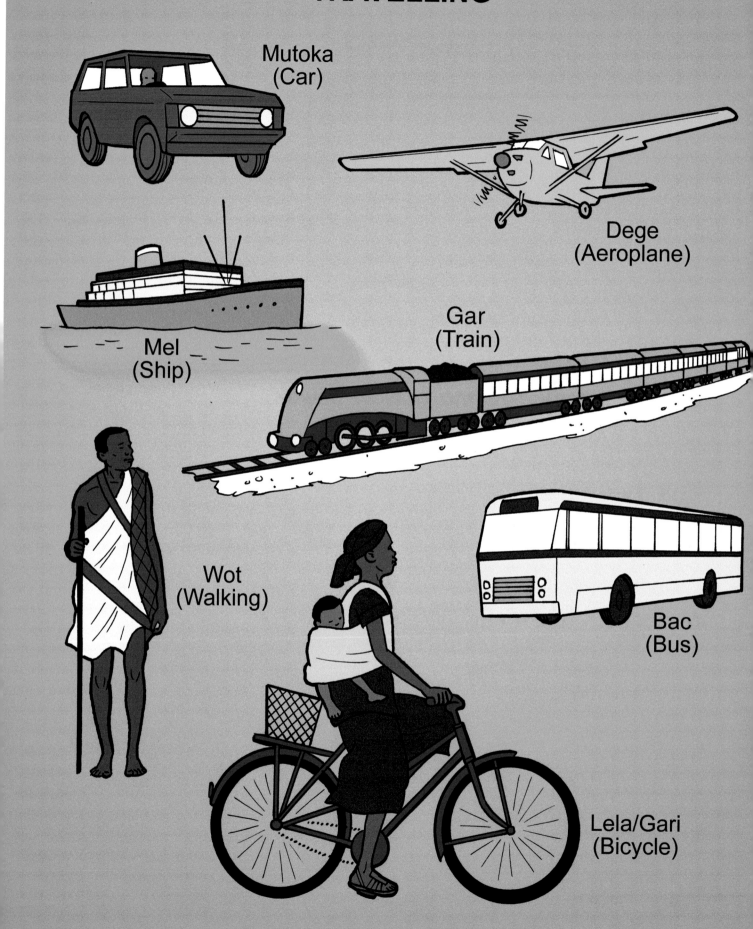

Bac tye kacero Kampala.
The bus is travelling to Kampala.

Gar woto oyot adada.
Trains are very fast.

Dege dit loyo mutoka.
Planes are bigger than cars.

Pud pe abedo I mel.
I have never been on a ship.

SCHOOL

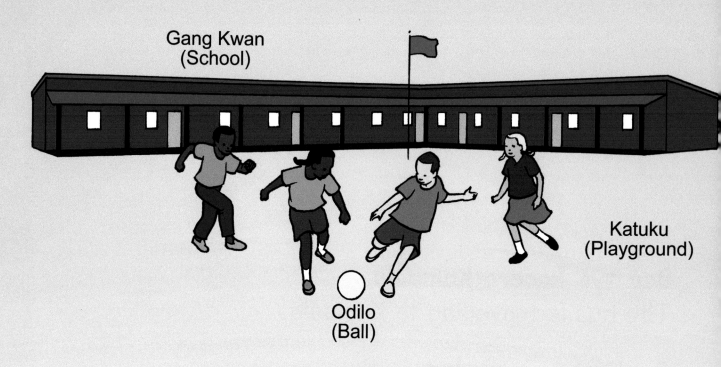

Gang Kwan
(School)

Katuku
(Playground)

Odilo
(Ball)

Ot kwan
(Classroom)

Bau coc
(Board)

ABC

Latin Kwan
(Student)

Kwan
(Read)

Choo
(Write)

Kom
(Chair)

Kalam
(Pen)

Meca
(Table/Desk)

Lapwony
(Teacher)

Buk
(Book)

En maro kwan.
He/She loves learning.

Lupwonye cwiny gi ber.
Teachers are kind.

Atuko ki larema.
I play with my friend.

Wa coyo I buk.
We wrote in the book.

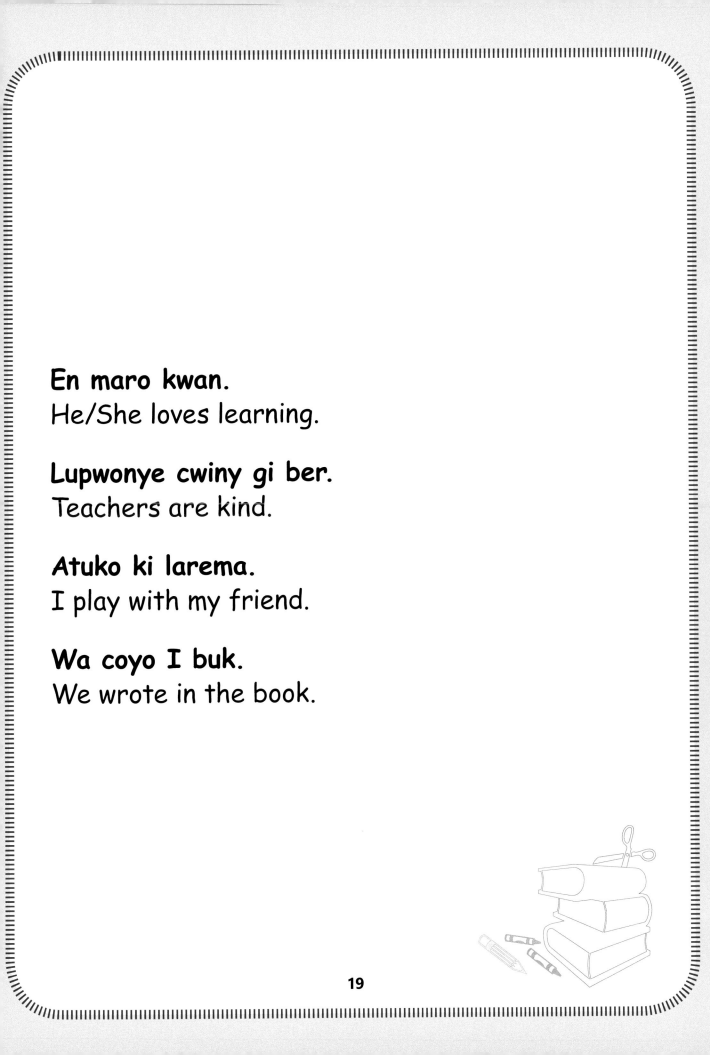

DRESSING

Long
(Trousers)

Otok
(Hat)

Cati
(Shirt)

War
(Shoes)

Tetei
(Dress)

Curuwal
(Short)

Coti
(Coat)

"*Gomesi*"
Gomci

Kanyi
(Tunic)

Ruk war ni.
Put on your shoes.

Cati ni dyak.
Your shirt is wet.

Miya otoki.
Give me your hat.

Lwok boni ni.
Wash your clothes.

CULTURE

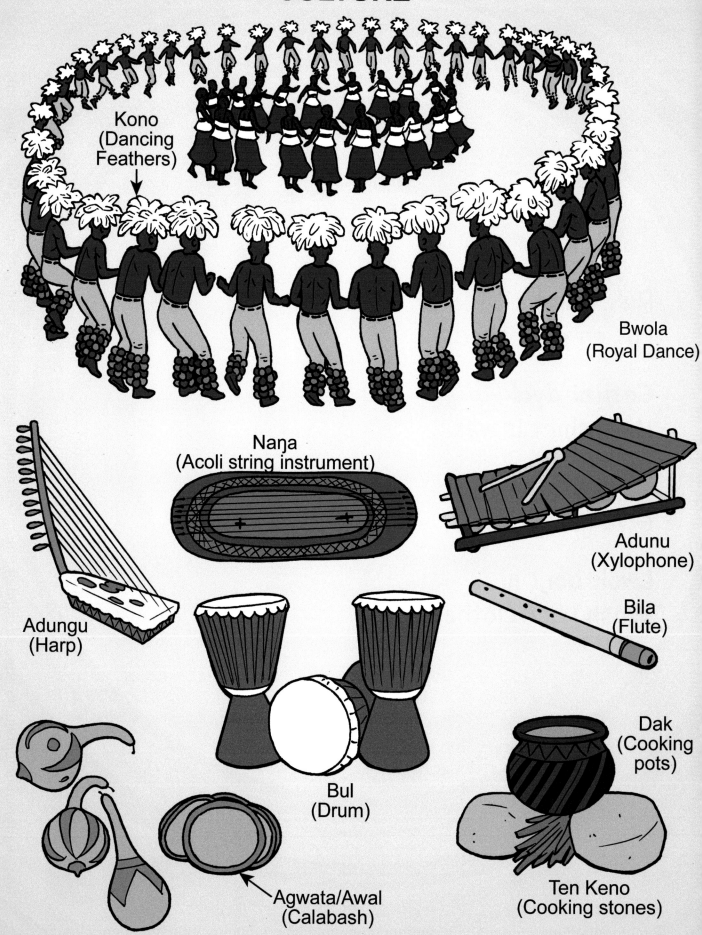

Kono (Dancing Feathers)

Bwola (Royal Dance)

Naŋa (Acoli string instrument)

Adunu (Xylophone)

Adungu (Harp)

Bila (Flute)

Bul (Drum)

Dak (Cooking pots)

Agwata/Awal (Calabash)

Ten Keno (Cooking stones)

Omera tye ka goyo bul.
My brother is playing drums.

Waya oturu dak keno.
My auntie broke the cooking pot.

Aŋeyo myello Larakaraka.
I can dance "Larakaraka".

Nera peke ki Agwata.
My uncle has no calabash.

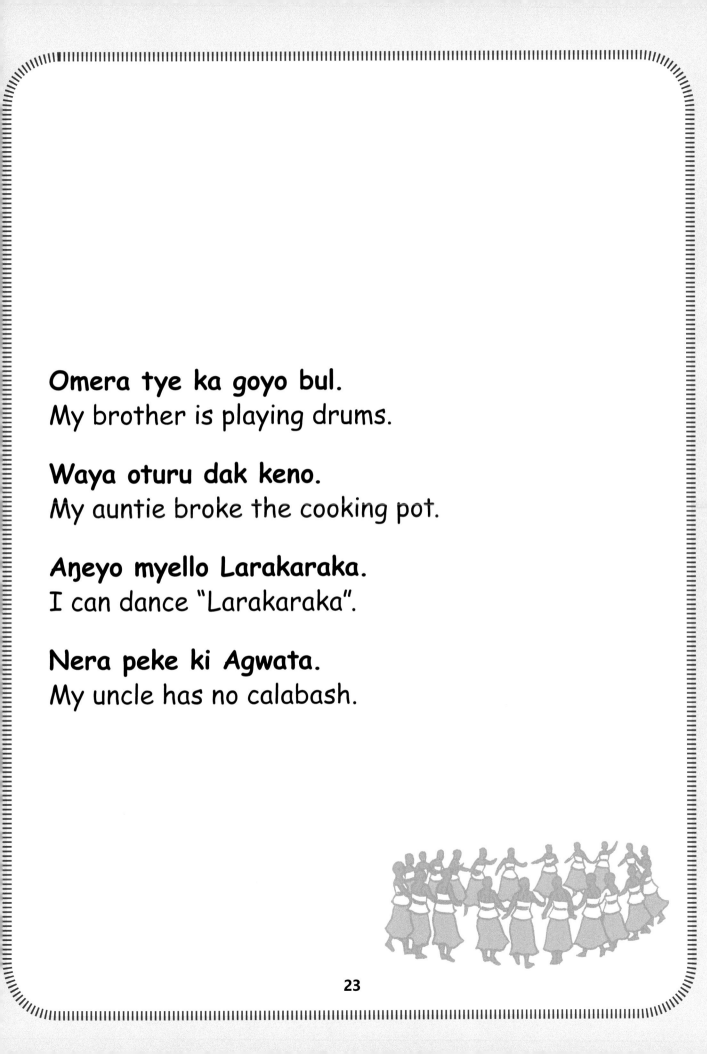

The song below is a children's play song. It can be sung when children are playing alone or with an adult. It talks about a young child remembering his/her love for a delicacy called "Malakwang" which is a vegetable made with peanut paste. They recall licking the bottom of the bowl after the meal.

Dek malakwang olel, ma an puda tidi,

Acidu mera te atabu, ma an puda atidi

Printed in the United States
By Bookmasters